WHERE THE MOON IS

Lois Welshons

LAUREL
POETRY
COLLECTIVE

ACKNOWLEDGMENTS

"That Week at the Mint Cafe" and "The Tuesday before Thanksgiving" previously appeared in *Voiceprint*; "The Familiar" in *Water~Stone* (Fall 2002); "Enough" in *A New Name for the Sun* (Laurel Poetry Collective, 2003); "Tapestry" in *Pulling for Good News* (Laurel Poetry Collective, 2004); "Zinnias" in *Bluefire* (Laurel Poetry Collective, 2005). "Loon" was set to letterpress broadside by Regula Russelle, Laurel Poetry Collective, 2003.

Epigraphs and other quoted excerpts: "Curriculum Vitae" by Lisel Mueller from *Alive Together* (Baton Rouge, LA: Louisiana University Press, 2002); untitled poem by Thomas McGrath from *Letters to Tomasita* (Duluth, MN: Holy Cow! Press, 1977); "Some People Like Poetry" and "I'm Working on the World" by Wisława Szymborska, translated from the Polish by Stanisław Barańczak and Clare Cavanagh, from *Poems New and Collected* (New York: Harcourt, 1988); "Wild Geese" by Mary Oliver from *New and Selected Poems* (Boston: Beacon Press, 1992); "Rothko" by Jim Moore from *The Freedom of History* (Minneapolis: Milkweed Editions, 1988); "But Something Is" by William Bronk from *Living Instead* (San Francisco: North Point Press, 1991).

Thanks to the ever-faithful Monday morning poetry group for their help in shaping many poems. I am especially grateful to my poet friends Yvette Nelson and Deborah Keenan for helping me with this book. And a final thank you to the Laurel Poetry Collective, of course: all of us committed to poetry and to sending each of our voices out to the world.

© 2005 by Lois Welshons

All rights reserved.

ISBN 0-9761153-5-2

Printed in the United States of America.

Published by Laurel Poetry Collective
1168 Laurel Avenue, St. Paul MN 55104

www.laurelpoetry.com

Book design and drawings by Sylvia Ruud

Library of Congress Cataloging-in-Publication Data

Welshons, Lois.
    Where the moon is / Lois Welshons.
        p. cm.
    ISBN 0-9761153-5-2 (alk. paper)
    I. Title.
PS3623.E483W47 2005
811'.6—dc22

2005019773

for John,
   always enough

CONTENTS

One

Desire fills the world	10
Unbidden	12
What Else	13
The Familiar	14
What Loneliness Does	15
A Friendship, Broken	16
To My Children	18
Retrieval	19
Longing	20
Border	21
Galliard	22

Two

Tapestry	24
Small Elegy	25

That Week at the Mint Cafe	26
Frenzy	28
With My Sister	29
The Color Version	30
Motives	31
The Tuesday before Thanksgiving	32
New Puzzle	34
What I Could Have Done	35
Curtain	36
Annual Family Reunion	37
The Family	38

Three

In our lives how slight the reason	40
Lynch Creek Dam in September	41
Enough	42
Because you are here	43
Grief	44
Weather Fronts	45
After diagnosis	46
Deserve	47
Spring Storm	48
Shift	50
Recovery	51
The Meaning of Blue	52

Four

Carnival	54
Loon	55
Trees	56
Moon	57
Attending the World	58
Teal Lake in Winter: Two Views	59
On Making Plans	60
Transition	61
The Story of My Life	62

Five

Claim	64
Real	65
Dusk	67
Daily I think about death	68
Passing	69
Hanging Around for God	70
Portraits in Time	72
Meditation	73
Zinnias	74
Do what you can	75
Happiness	76
Landscape: Self-Portrait	77

One

So far, so good. The brilliant days and nights are
breathless in their hurry. We follow, you and I.

—Lisel Mueller, "Curriculum Vitae"

Desire fills the world

Dragonflies dart   hover   flit
    make quick work
of mosquitoes, accept gratitude
    secretly want
admiration (those silver filigree wings)

Shadows love their shifty life,
    their long stretches
as evening comes on, their
only worry a solid bank of clouds

Wind insists it merely wants to caress our skin
    sift through leaves
but its temper flares, thrashes trees
    lifts entire villages
then subsiding feigns innocence

Whatever is vague thinks that's best for us
    so it pats our hand
and hums a tune no one can identify

Head (always level) seeks to negotiate peace
    with wild heart
but every day heart comes to the table late
quarrels over terms, forever ups the ante

Scrabble forces a choice: seek
    a serviceable word
on a triple-word square   instead go for
    sarong or *ennui*
point consequences be damned?

Common oxeye, feverfew, hoary vervain:
        capable prairie sisters
feet planted deep survive dry soil, sun scorch
ask only for the occasional incineration

The older we become the more we desire all
        the presence in absence
the more we hope that some One will contain us

Unbidden

                Now and again
a moment enlarges: on the dock
at dawn maybe, coffee steaming,
whiffets of air nudging mist
from the island out front,
or perhaps in the garden,
shadows green, a bird not seen
over and over chanting *chee chee*
until even your hold-back heart
lets go.
                But not now
having come from the store where
the strawberries were picked over
and someone cut in front of you
at the checkout, not now driving down
this small-town street, sun nearly gone,
the remarkable redness of brakes flashing
on the car ahead, *Speed Limit 25 Miles*
perfectly articulated, food wrappers nestled
next to the curb, and your car cleverly rounds
a corner, heads home through an immense ordinary.

What Else

What else heaven does not contain are
small groups: those assigned assemblages
fumbling for focus, the wholly
inaccurate report to the larger group,
the cheery leader's indiscriminate approval

Also no grand opera, especially Wagnerian
bloated with public lamentation
that glut of artifice (this exception—
an occasional aria arising like
smoke from a smoldering heart)

Nothing in pieces or partial,
no one turned into a pitted olive,
mind sucked out and flung
God knows where, cavity stuffed with
fear on bad days, oblivion on good

Left behind, too, our tiresome
pronouncements, sureties about God,
words can't be heard anyway
over the clamor of silent joy
and heaven only knows what else

The Familiar

Because we love how it fends off the terrors,
   because it gets us from morning to night,
     we pull it close,

let it surround us, wrap tight around us—
   how will we know we've nearly
     stopped breathing,

our skin now paling and eyesight failing
   under this cover we've drawn
     over lessening lives,

performing our daily ritual, the habitual
   avoidance of gamble, automatic
     murder of chance.

What Loneliness Does

Like a windowpane that separates the silent gray interior from the streaming outside street, loneliness is a tease. Eager to show off the world to you—the top of that oak tree nodding amiably to the green ash; cars crisscrossing city streets, speeding down freeways, all heading toward places where someone expects them—but it muffles all sound. Lips move, bodies hunch forward in what seems to be laughter. Even if you managed to pry the window open, the words seem unknowable, a foreign language you didn't study hard enough.

You're glad your agony is private, though animals can't be fooled. (You emit an odor like damp dust.) Dogs follow you, flop at your feet, gaze in pity. Cats of course seize opportunity. They curl up on your lap, know you're paralyzed, incapable of throwing them off, even though their deep throaty purr annoys you and rattles the solitary teacup that's been sitting there for days next to that photograph of people with fakey smiles, shoulders pressed stupidly together.

A Friendship, Broken

Days passed before I even noticed
how the glass had fallen from my hand
that afternoon, exploded into countless jagged

pieces that shot across the kitchen floor.
Catching on, stupefied by her pointed silence,
I pulled on sturdy shoes and protective

gloves, gathered up the larger pieces,
hastily deposited them in the trash.
The shards that remained took months

to sweep up. Some lodged deep
in my throat, wouldn't budge,
ached by day, festered in the night.

Some took possession of my mind,
muttering *but* and *then you said*
and *never* and *how could you say*

until I grew nauseous from repetition.
I hesitated to tell people about the broken
glass—for so many years they'd admired it:

its extra-thick base, the complicated
etched patterns circling,
no apparent beginning, no likely endings.

I would search faces for sympathy.
Did they think I'd been careless?
Worse, to blame? (With each retelling

my story stayed true, yet was a trifle
more polished, to reflect better on me.
It's so tempting, so easy—a word

weighted, an incident construed this way,
or that.) Some people knew the glass
was nicked and chipped, even

deeply cracked, would say it was only
a matter of time anyway. Was it?
Some days I think back over the years,

how my arm had grown weary
from holding it, and I can admit
I may have loosened,

a little, my grip, shifted just
one finger maybe, enough so that
the glass plummeted, shattered

irreparably. All these years later,
I still occasionally step barefoot
on a splinter I missed

in the sweeping up, some days of pain
until it's worked its way out. And then
there's this: how I never tried to glue

the pieces back together. Will that
omission be fatal, ruining eternity
for me? I picture myself showing off

for God my small cupboard, its several
rows of glasses, each one cherished,
a few mended, but God just frowns hard

at the empty space.

To My Children

I didn't even mention you
when I wrote "The Story of My Life."

>It's not that I've forgotten you.
>Some winter dusks
>I look from my kitchen window
>and I see your shadows
>hurrying up the long, icy drive
>and in an instant, I think,
>you'll burst in the door,
>yell *Mom?*
>ask what's for supper,
>drop your books on the floor,
>presume your place, your welcome.
>
>Always the kitchen stays still,
>the door unopened,
>the clock is ticking, ticking.
>Drifts as deep, as heavy
>as absence
>surround this house.
>
>Down from the big blue spruce
>in our blue-black yard
>the snow is sifting, sifting.

Retrieval

How tempting it is
to escape
like a runaway horse
leaping the fences
or a restless bird
leaving a line-up
too close on the wire

How easy it is
to come back
when a granddaughter says
Nana, sometimes
we need help
reaching the ketchup,
don't we?

Longing

surges dark within me
March water
restive
under a thin skim of ice

propels me into dusky streets
sidelong glances
at lighted windows
perfect lives

stupefies with regrets
wordless
when most
I want to speak

It ambushes me in photographs
sturdy smile
outsize front teeth
once my little boy

It turns me a fool for yearning
geranium
in the basement
straining for the sun

tightens fingers around my throat
car at the corner
tiny last wave
gone

It lures me unsuspecting
Chopin nocturne
silken light
ageless smell of cinnamon

Longing confounds me deepest in the night
missing you
though your dear body
lies close, so warm

Border

So porous the border here, September undetected
slips into August: dims down the green and flips
on yellow, stretches soft white veils over land

lying low, places two red leaves on the patio.
August is unperturbed—the way close relatives
overlook presumption—plots a future foray

in the company of diligent bees, clouds of gnats,
the rocking summer sun on a farewell tour.
Before long, with little notice, we ourselves

will slip out of time, leave behind place, hope
audacious assumptions meet unending grace.

Galliard

> ...patterns that only the casual eye,
> lazy with joy, can find
> —Jim Moore, "Rothko"

As if you could catch up
when already you're late for early
vegetables—the ones that drink
deep the cool spring rains,
wilt slow in a full-tilt sun—so
you hurry: grab trowel and
claw, gloves, seeds, onion sets,
new markers for the rows;
haul composted cow manure,
turn the soil, work it in,
is that the murmur of worms?
work you love, cardinals call,
breathe the blossoming plums,
don't stop until you collapse
on the bench to make a plan,
feel a familiar, small regret
you'd made no record of last
year's garden,
                    and you see
two squirrels leap and race
atop the garden fence, stopped
now face to face. One advances,
one retreats, then they reverse
their tiny, quick steps, forward
and back, over, then over again,
their backyard galliard
the way daily you step
out to the world, the world
dances back into you.

Two

How could I have come so far?
...I must have traveled by the light
Shining from the faces of all those I have loved.

—Thomas McGrath, untitled poem

Tapestry

My parents are woven into a tapestry
called Courtly Love on the Prairie.
Her long gown is unadorned
since he could give her no jewels.
She sits serene on the dais
where early he placed her.
She bends to study the holy, illuminated text
that lies open on her lap.
He, a village tradesman, kneels before his lady,
content in admiration.

> Just when I want to
> slam the book shut
> and lift the edge of her gown
> to see her ordinary feet,
> she vanishes in the night.

He stays in place, kneeling for years.
At mere mention of her name, he weeps,
each tear a jewel, glistening.

Small Elegy

I remember the mania
of mumblety-peg,
June morning playing
in my mind, old movie
rerun, this screenplay:
throaty call of doves
summer morning sound
grass tipped with dew
sparkles, ten-year-old girl
told to stay inside in case
mother calls from bedroom
slips out back door, careful
not to let it slam, heads for
best spot under Chinese elm,
pulls jackknife from pocket
squats, flips knife off one big
toe, then the other, twists to
do her heels, moves up body
flicking knife from every
body part she's allowed to
name, glad no one's around to
argue whether two fingers fit
under slant of knife, loves clean
straight-up landings—slice!
slice! squats, starts over
wonders if there's such a thing
as the mumblety-peg queen
repeats routine, hears nothing
until the ambulance, terrified
to see mother on stretcher
nurse says she'll be okay
father not scolding

Dissolve to
knife put away
dove in mourning
sound of childhood
running down

That Week at the Mint Café

When I am in third grade,
my dad takes me with him
for a plate dinner at the Mint Café,
every noon for a whole week.
My mother, I'm told, is having
a little female trouble taken care of
in the Home Hospital.

The mornings in school are maddening.
We loiter through endless multiplication tables,
and Palmer-method circles, and "White Coral Bells,"
until I can spring for the cloakroom.
The indulgent January sun flings
diamonds helter-skelter on the snow before me.
I skim across the snow's hard crust,
running to meet my father,
who waits at the Mint Café,
a knight in a storm coat
standing by that palace door.

The crowd of farmers and storekeepers
around the two horseshoe counters
are laughing and smoking and
shaking dice for their coffee.
They lift and turn their heads
as we pass,
smile at my dad and me.
Someone calls out, "Hey, C. G., who's your girlfriend?"
My dad jokes back: "I don't know,
but she sure is good-looking, isn't she?"
He winks at me and together we slide
into a booth gleaming with varnish,
its back as tall as a throne.

The men turn back to their games.
They talk and laugh, laugh and talk,
and so do the clever, busy waitresses,
and so do the oranges in the Orange Crush sign.

We eat roast beef and mashed potatoes,
a moat of rich, brown gravy
encircling them on the plate.
My father doesn't mention
the pale green beans I'm ignoring.
He doesn't talk much at all.
I keep my eye on the big front window,
sheeted over with steam.
Occasionally a drop of water forms
near the top and rolls downward
in tiny fits and starts,
leaving behind a blurry trail.

Each day when the waitress comes to take our plates,
my dad says to her, "Bet I know someone
who'd like some ice cream."
But on Friday when the waitress comes,
my dad, acting happy,
adds that we won't be back next week—
my mother is coming home.
I turn down the ice cream.

Frenzy

Once in a while
we'd spot her
down the street

we never knew
who made
the ruling: this

strange one is
fair game even
for children

but we'd taunt her
circle
hurl a few stones

then of a sudden
we'd scatter
to our separate backyards

sit silent at supper
never mention
our frenzy of fun

With My Sister

It is winter in the afternoon.
We sit together in the sidelong sun,
my big sister and me. My legs dangle

off the bench by the dressing table
with the ruffly skirt tacked on.
I get to touch the Evening in Paris set

someone named Jack gave her
before he went away to The War.
The box is shaped like a heart.

Inside is white satin, with little
beds for the perfume bottle,
the box of powder. I feel

the bottle's deep dark blue,
not like any blue I've got
in my crayons, a blue I think

only Paris gets to have.
I ask to have some powder.
My sister lets me lift out

the box, take off the lid.
She picks up the puff,
says to hold out my arms,

then she pats them softly
up and down. Little powdery
clouds float in the sidelong sun,

drift down into the years ahead:
clouds, arms reaching out,
winter and deeper, deeper blue,

white satin lines her bed.

The Color Version

From the beginning, black and white. Baby girl strains
to balance on someone's knee. Small girl stands straight,
knees together, frowns into the sun.

Nothing for years. No money, no time. The whole country
black and white, *Let Us Now Praise Famous Men*, Okies
stream to California, railroad beds scoured for coal.

Summer 1945, lots of photos at a lake cottage, still they're
black and white. My sister and her girl friends vamp and pose
languorously on the dock, Betty Grable pin-ups in ruffled,
polka-dotted two-piecers. They look happy. The Boys will
be home soon. My sister does not look unhappy, but still
she has a hard time with the sun.

Years in a nun's habit. Black skirt to the floor,
white wimple circling a serious face. Some blurry color
photos now, but always my sister black and white.

Then five frantic years. Looking for love
where it couldn't be found. Said we were her bridge
over troubled water, but her waters were black
and rose too high and who could ever bridge them?

Last letter: said she was okay, wrote how
she loved the red geranium on her windowsill,
how it turned toward the sun.

Motives

A certain directness pervades these Northwoods.
The local eagle drops down from his pine
and the ducks that swim below don't loiter.
Jonquils by the fence push through matted leaves,
intent on a single week of perfect yellow.
Hundreds of frogs scream *please oh please*,
fill the dusk with their shameless pleading.

When a quarter century ago our sister
killed herself in San Francisco, my two brothers
and I conspired to keep the cause of death
a secret from our elderly father. A virulent pneumonia,
we told him, and all the others in our small town.
We only wanted to save our beloved father
from the particular grief that follows suicide.
All along he had his doubts, but we held fast.
It's taken me years to see the real duplicity,
how ashamed we were, how proud.

The Tuesday before Thanksgiving

How could they have known,
that Tuesday before Thanksgiving?

They ate their supper as usual in the blue dinette,
mentioning this and that.
They listened to the weather on WCCO:
sleet likely, turning to snow.
Maybe the worst of it will be over
by Thanksgiving, they said to one another.
He wandered off to the living room,
settled down with his paper in the big, rose, friezed chair.
From long habit he dozed off,
letting the paper slip out of his hands
and slide to the floor.
She stayed in the kitchen alone,
putting leftovers into the refrigerator,
washing up their few dishes,
wiping the counters.
Might as well get a jump on the holiday
and make up that Peach Party Salad right now.
She put water in a pan to boil for the jello,
then assembled the ingredients
for her favorite special-occasion salad.

He never heard the explosion in the kitchen,
slept right through it.
And she too was unaware.
She heard only the faint tapping of sleet on the windows
as she moved about her kitchen,
opening the peaches,
chopping some walnuts,
absently popping a maraschino cherry into her mouth.

No way they could have known,
on Tuesday before Thanksgiving,
that while he dozed
and she made Peach Party Salad,
an arterial explosion
muffled deep in her brain
had ripped them apart forever.

New Puzzle

I am eight,
sitting beside my dad
at holy High Mass.

Men in Sunday suits thrust long-handled baskets
down each pew
to catch the dollar bills.
My empty stomach rumbles.

Sanctus! Sanctus! Sanctus!
Bells ring.
Kneelers crash.

I listen to the Latin prayers
until Father's voice starts to fade,
flames leave their candles.

Why is Dad carrying me?
Where am I?
Then I hear someone say,
"Look, she's a frightened deer!"
and it's *Sanctus!* again,
new puzzle to ponder:
   how I am still myself,
    and yet I am a deer.

What I Could Have Done

Until that winter in Harlingen, Texas,
my father had traveled outside Minnesota
only three times in seventy-eight years.
He lay unconscious when I got there,
respirator tube gurgling in his throat,
antibiotics mainlined to his drowning lungs.

For a week, I stood by his bed.
I got used to his bare, white, heaving chest,
but never the tan
on forearms and neck, too exotic
for this Minnesota man in February.

At the time, all I could think to do for him
was rub his shoulders, hold his hand.
Not easy to do.
He was deeply agitated,
shifting and turning constantly,
sometimes flipping his entire body into the air,
frantic as any fish out of water.

It's clear to me now, Father,
what I could have done
to ease your dying.
How I wish I'd lifted you
in omnipotent arms
and carried you down the elevator
and out the hospital door
and stepped over Oklahoma
and run across Nebraska
and laid you down
gently
in your shiny frozen garden
in the southwest corner
of Minnesota.

—with thanks to Robert Francis

Curtain

I. I am supposed to be napping but I am four and I lift the curtain to peek out at my big brothers, who have jackknives and baseball bats and can buy pop at the gas station five blocks away.

II. My best friend and I pin her mom's old blue taffeta curtains around our waists, dance on the back of the big stone fireplace in her backyard. We twirl umbrellas on our shoulders and sing "I'm Looking Over a Four-Leaf Clover." The blue taffeta curtains know what later we'll learn: the shimmer's set off by the shadowy folds.

III. Saturday nights we make popcorn, play pranks on the telephone. We tell the operator made-up numbers and when someone answers, we say, "Help, help! Pop's in the cooler and can't get out." So clever we snort with laughter. After awhile Central tears away anonymity. "You kids, cut it out or I'll tell your mom."

IV. Ta-da! Presenting the Fantastic Fifties, starring: The Bomb. The Fear. The Iron Curtain.

V. In my bedroom, priscillas, of course. Over and over I play my favorite, "Once I Had a Secret Love," sit in the window hoping I will see my best friend's brother walk by. So sweet: the curtains, the agony.

VI. Our two young daughters drape themselves in sheer white curtains, flit about under the oaks. They say, "Look, we're Egyptian princesses." The sun is setting and I say they are beautiful white birds I cannot hold onto.

VII. My husband takes his elderly mother out for rides, holds her hand as they drive. One day she says, "Tell me, John, how's your mother?" He turns to her. "But *you're* my mother." "Well, then, you must have two," she chirrups. Always resilient, but not strong enough to hold back the thick curtain closing.

Annual Family Reunion

We gather again.
>This perennial garden, wild profusion of the
>years: bright showy flowers that bask in fullest
>sun, the many quiet seekers of shade and cover,
>those sturdy border guards vigilant against
>onslaught of the shrewd and cunning lawn.
>We all know where we belong; stems lean
>toward one another, leaves stretch to touch,
>we hold one another up by mere presence,
>the fondest expectations.

Some stories, some silences.
>Bleeding heart with crimson tears. Pushy,
>spreading purple loosestrife. Lily so pale
>it's disappearing. Circles of primrose, tidy,
>contained. Narcissus turned upon itself.
>Bittersweet, the bittersweet.

We plan for our return.
>O spare this garden winterkill: the bare,
>black earth, tiny cries in the summer night,
>an unspeakable   space   among us.

The Family

dark woods from which we stagger
brambles trailing

favorite old toy
   paint chipped
   parts missing

an irresistible bug light
   zzzzzzzst!

the urgent-care clinic
open 24 hours
pre-authorization not required

a drama in countless acts
surprise entrances
all those final exits

holy wholly sanctuary
incense of sweet acceptance
remembrances rising

sidewalk-sale grab bag

a theme with variations
   the comfort of repetition
   the delights of aberration

ghosts
spin in the backyard,
plotting to take over the house

Three

...I just keep on not knowing and I cling to that like a redemptive handrail.

—Wisława Szymborska, "Some People Like Poetry"

In our lives how slight the reason

that we will choose
this person, not that one

More than once you've
mentioned that night

getting to know each other
talking about our families

you told me *My father
never said I love you*

and I instantly outraged
for the boy you once were

and you so startled to consider
for the first time

it wasn't your fault
could not have been

Was that for you
the unseen moment

this small redress
weighty enough

to hold and press
your life to mine?

Lynch Creek Dam in September

We'd relinquished summer,
after a week of winds from the north.
Now we're pulling sweatshirts off
as we emerge from the woods, drop
our bodies on the edge of the pond
formed when the creek got dammed.
We sit separate in the shoreline weeds,
the only sound the pines
shifting in the light southerly breeze.
A turtle is stretched across a rock
lifting its neck to the sun.
Bees attach to the goldenrod.
You move close,
touch the skin on the back of my neck.
The ground is still warm,
the air shot with autumn spices.
Then this: a long intimacy of hands and years.
The water's surface shudders and
the turtle lets go the rock,
slides fast and deep
to a lovely hidden place.

Enough

Am I not enough? you ask, aloud this time.
It's early morning at the cabin.
A dozen or more evening grosbeaks,
a football team in yellow and black jerseys,
swoop down from the pines between us

and the lake, shoulder each other for
sunflower seeds on the feeding tray.
These birds never show up in the evening:
Audubon's error, or just timing gone awry?
It's come up again, my discontent, unnamable

and tenacious, as it so often does
when the two of us put a measure
to our lives, as we've done together
for over thirty years. Yes, yes, I say,
of course you're enough. Half of me

means it and half of you believes it.
I look past the pines, toward the lake.
What if later I discover my timing was off:
when your warmth next to me, your wide soul
that accommodates this tedium, are gone.

Because you are here

Steady drum of summer rain
blocks my soul's thrum of pain
because you are here.

Plaintive moans in summer breeze
languish to song, desire to please
because you are here.

Wanton cries of crow and jay
rouse me now to chance what may
because you are here.

Grief

I feel its dark presence again,
look up from this garden
we two have tended for years,
rearranging perennials,
assessing bloom-time,
color, all the incidentals
lucky accidentals
of what's become
a sturdy garden, a marriage
lovely beyond the first dream.

I glare and it pulls back
behind the thorny locust,
but not completely out of sight.
It's grown bolder
now that time is on its side,
loiters in wait for death
to choose between us,
that moment
this assailant's cue
to make its move, possess
the other for itself.

Weather Fronts

Only a few times in my life
I've been in the right geographic spot
and sufficiently aware even to notice:
how air one minute is calm, silent

then, no warning,
it's wind, scatters
leaves, moans in the trees,
slams a door.

I've grown more alert with age.
Now as I sit with friends, drinking
wine in the uneventful sunshine,
I listen for the sound

of a cell going berserk,
a heart improvising its beat,
the tiny slap of blood
against arterial plaque.

After diagnosis

Once there was a single word spoken
so huge it swallows all air, blocks the exits.
It yanks off its clever disguises,
creeps steady as a crab, seventh sign of the sun.

All day the perfect summer sun mocks.
Birds sing in the locust, oblivious
to the shadows inside, how they wander
from room to room, stagger under the word.

Roads are still full of cars speeding
here and there, riders looking forward
to their destinations. We cannot flee.
We do not know where to go.

Deserve

I. We construct a world according to merit.
    Tames the chaos, allows some control.

    We categorize the poor among us,
    want our alms bestowed on the deserving.

    We assess the worthiness of Powerball winners,
    loved the school cafeteria workers in red T-shirts,
    congenial women vowing to keep their humble jobs.

    And we're not easily fooled, either.
    Dress like that and you're asking for it.

    One good turn deserves another, we say.
    (Same goes for bad ones, too, of course.
    Three cheers for the death penalty!
    Blessed are the revenge-takers.)

    Told someone has died of lung cancer,
    Instantly we want to know: *Did he smoke?*

    Well, she had a long life anyway, we murmur,
    as if death's entitled to its easy takedowns.

    Obituaries will heap praise on the long,
    courageous battle with death. Never a
    good word for the short, terrified skirmish.

II. Sun is said to shine
    alike on the good, the bad;
    random too the rain.

    We did not deserve
    three red birds at the feeder;
    they, the strike of hawk.

Spring Storm

Lightning. Direct hit. Warning signs missed.

Doctors rush in and out of his room, page through the thickening chart, shake their heads. The next few days will be crucial, they say. Day after day.

It is spring. The skies low and gray, rain frequent and cold.

Drip and gasp of the IV pump. Tiny medicinal soldiers dispatched around the clock. What chance do they have arrayed against the bacterial hordes coursing now through brain and spine?

The children hold her up, hold each other up. One son-in-law weeps standing at the foot of the bed, the other in her arms. Friends, that other family, surround them.

A doctor confides, Worst case I've ever seen.

He's been gone for weeks now. She doesn't know if he'll ever return. He tells her he's on a runaway boat on the Mississippi, or in a restaurant and no one will take his order, or he can't crawl out of a huge upside-down umbrella. The cathedral dome, rising real outside his window, is sinister; the clock on the wall not to be trusted. He begs her to cover them up.

She resents the springtime joggers. He can barely lift one leg, cannot lift the other at all. He may never walk again.

She walks in a waking nightmare, her only escape to tumble deep into blank sleep.

Crisis after crisis. You're a very complicated guy, they say to him. Is that praise? she wonders. Chastisement? Perhaps, she thinks, they're preparing me.

Once, in a moment of seeming lucidity, he asks her, Should we give up? She shakes her head, speech impossible. All day she worries, Am I asking too much?

Please, please, please. Is that a prayer? Anyone listening? She's willing to do anything. Anything.

The house is dark when she comes home, silent in the dawn. (Except for that morning when loud wails break loose from somewhere deep inside and for what seems a long time she wanders from room to room, wringing her hands, howling.)

One night she says it out loud to friends. I don't think he will live. No one disputes her.

With summer, the skies change, remind her of a Constable painting full as they are every day with huge, billowing clouds (herself the tiny, inconsequential figure traveling under them).

SHIFT

For our children

Our son, faithful bearer of Starbucks,
not naturally given to seeing
life's cup half-full, searches out small
signs of hope. He offers them to me,
like the dandelions when he was little.

One daughter arranges friends,
other family to sit with her father,
hoping I'll leave for an hour or two.
Brings nutritious snacks from her co-op,
rich sustenance from her heart.

Another daughter wheels in
with her newborn, nurses him,
changes him, sits and sits with me,
places his small perfect body
in my arms. Life. See life.

They sit vigil in the Family Room,
so I'll know they're close by,
would hear me if I called to them.

They appear in the doorway,
backlit by light spilling in from the hall,
come to comfort in this desolate night.

Recovery

I arrive in the night, make small deals in molecules, my notable guile
erratic

zigzagging, the flicker of a firefly. Coax me, I might reconcile
the key accounts:

damaged cells dispatched, replacements then recruited. I arrive
as permitted,

scheduled by mystery, and if I wish—last resort!—I'll contrive
a dream:

grasses green as—well, grass—clouds perched on horizon—
this standard still

sufficient to cause hesitation, refocus an errant eye on
this world.

The Meaning of Blue

Not low moan of a Kansas City saxophone.
Not a sagging spirit, nothing to cure it.
Forget blue skies smiling at me,
nothing but blue skies do I see.

Weeks of clouds, earth in shrouds,
you're all but resigned, little hope in mind
then here   over there   now disappear
reappear BLUE BLUE BLUE so clear

so undeserved—some clouds had swerved,
let slivers show through, your first clue
that recovery might follow, this intaglio
in clouds revealing out-of-the-blue healing.

Four

Whoever you are, no matter how lonely,
the world offers itself
to your imagination.

—Mary Oliver, "Wild Geese"

CARNIVAL

I do not know a carnival
has come to town until after supper
when my dad asks, Want to go
downtown with me? but there it is
stretching the two blocks of Main Street
from The Fashionette and the locker plant
at one end, all the way down to Worthmore Dairy.
My dad holds my hand and I ride the merry-go-round
and people say hello to my dad and he buys me a
bottle of Crème Soda at the Knights of Columbus
and the evening sky darkens, carnival lights sparkle,
and we ride the Ferris wheel together three times and
at the top we can see the moon rising
pale with envy at the edge of the prairie
struck dumb by carnival.

Loon

        regulars envy him   minimalist
          in crisp black and white   (floating
              New York restaurant riding low in the water)
           oh-so-artfully-placed
      ruby   red   eye

     up from the Gulf   taking over
    the northern lakes   cries resound
shore to shore   open-throttle
        voice   territorial shrieks   maniacal
          laughter   (even Webster's calls it weird)

   how we love loon's haunting wail
  reverberating   reverberating
across our darkened lake   though the year-arounds
(bear, deer, fox)   narrow their eyes at his call
     think it not fair   can it possibly be
this loud transient's the favored one   appointed
     to conjure our northern dream: green-black
         spires of pine lining a shore   the slap slap   slap
            of boat

Trees

Trees in secret trace the years,
circle themselves with record
of rain, suffer a saw to tell the story.
Trees let families stash their past.
And some trees, in December's dark,
will pour forth into our homes
their fragrant green souls.

Given half a chance trees will
follow every curve of earth, pop up
on every horizon, insinuate themselves
into the tiniest crevice of a heart.
Ecstasy of trees is a common
disease and highly contagious.
Expose yourself.

Trees, with ease, partition the people.
The pulse of some quickens
as buds begin to bulge,
races in high tempo when
green explodes, then thickens.
Others favor the slow letting go,
savor partings, the pianissimo.

MOON

Heavy on the horizon

snared in a tangle of trees

moon breaks free

    perfect circle

    drifter

lingers close to darkened earth

lodges deep in our dreams.

By dawn moon is high

and pale, distant

wants to possess

nothing, cannot remember

anyone's dream. Moon

(even moon)

is not constant.

Attending the World

She embraces its materiality:
thrust of her legs pumping a bike,
flow of lake water over her naked body,
how beer cools a mouth alive with chili peppers.

He likes to supply the pesky, little-known
fact, lay out the latest theory, is visibly
comforted by the
linear exactitude of history.

And this friend picks up the slightest human
vibration, can be laid flat by ambiance,
must work to hold her own melody
over any room's emotional cacophony.

Mediocre in these ways, a little arrogant,
I make impossible demands, strain to see
an overlay of meaning, the interplay
of this fact and that
emotion and those sensations,
glumly aware that while I fret
the sun's past noon, soon will set.

Teal Lake in Winter: Two Views

1   The beginning is benign:
       Winter sun blithe in a thin blue sky.
       The woods anointed with watery light.
       My boots sharp against the frozen snow,
       the sound so seductive
       I walk on for miles.
    It's when I stop to rest
       I hear in that sudden silence
       the awful thudding of a solitary heart.
       I notice the sky has fallen into sullen gray,
       is seeping down between the trees.
    I've been in these woods long enough.

2   We sprawl around the fire on this aching winter night.
    These friends of ours are not brand-new,
    intriguing for what we don't yet know of them.
    These dear friends go way back, before King crumpled
    on that balcony and the second Kennedy was shot.
    Then childbirth and Vietnam and dope and family deaths
    and adolescent children—beyond the weddings now.
    I know what *cherish* means.

    These burnished piney walls, this vaulted ceiling
    hold us safe against the slicing cold.
    The bookcases bulge with Audubon guides, a sprinkling
    of classics, the cheery yellow of *Geographics*.
    The fire hisses. I rise to fetch the coffee pot.

    In the kitchen I hear it—a crack
    as loud as a gunshot.
    Ice is shifting on the roof.
    I look across the moonlit yard
    to the edge of those shadowy woods.
    I could reach them in a moment,
    vanish into solitude.

On Making Plans

Moth	Black-eyed Susan	Marten
Suffers tiny knicks	Perennial	Taste of mouse
along wing edges,	neighbors look	on tongue
leaves powdery	a little askance	marten inches
residue, proof	but she	forward
of desire	heedless	every muscle
	lets go	taut
	her seed	sudden squirrel
	to chance,	chittering
	trusts	and marten slumps
	the wisdom	random has rescued
	in shifting winds,	the dinner
	the rain's	he sought
	erratic dance	

Transition

For your last transition you'd prefer something
more thoughtful, slow.
Like the way music uses a few modulating chords
to move from minor mode to major,
some elements of both sounding together.
Or the way day eases into night,
holding onto shreds of light
until prepared to let them go, drift from sight.

Couldn't heaven have a vestibule?
A place to linger a while,
not required to wipe off traces of earth
clinging to your shoes, no one coaxing you inside
until you were ready. And this time no amnesia,
blotting out the scent of orange, flicker of fire,
the way mist moves over a lake.

The Story of My Life

When I was told to nap at age two or three, I looked out the window, and now years later I'm still looking out the window. I see trees tossing silently, no sound, and a biker turning the corner. I long. No answer. I long. Then I met a friend and I walked into his arms and now I look at him and he is burnished and glowing and it is what I know of him and love of him that lends the shine, soft shimmer. Words and words and words, and I toss them in the air and pluck them out one by one as it suits my fancy, and I string them and stack them and throw them from a cliff. They weigh me down, they fling me free. What spirit can I find? What meaning will there be? Not oblivion, I pray. To whom? For what? I see a shadow, not dark, but white, so white. Can I follow a white shadow?

Five

I'm working on the world,
revised, improved edition,
featuring fun for fools,
blues for brooders,
combs for bald pates,
tricks for old dogs.

—Wisława Szymborska,
"I'm Working on the World"

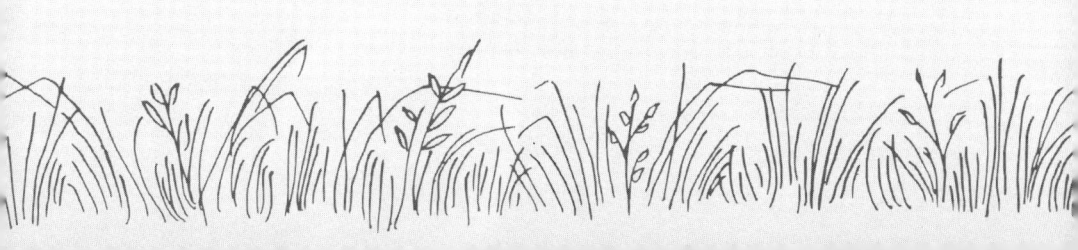

Claim

They're crazed to grasp the world,
possess it name by name:
cracker, baby, ball, bird.
They study their books,
announce what they find—
sun, dog, cow, tree—
glance over for
our confirming smiles.
Won't lie down in their cribs
at night until objects in sight
are labeled, given their name.
These granddaughters are doing their job.

And who can dispute the value of names?
Who of us wants a nameless disease,
an unnamed assailant, or fear?
Isn't psychology's mantra
"name it, you own it"?

I'm sick of naming.
After all these years
specificity has lost its appeal.
I want to let these brooding winter clouds
cross the sky unnamed, grant to
trees the mystery they crave.
Peel all labels off.
Be myself claimed
by the not named.

Real

> *It's what we mean as the real world.*
> *We don't get beyond it most days*
> *or even feel there is a real beyond.*
> —William Bronk, "But Something Is"

I know what's real,
meaning what "has permanence;
won't some day rot, collapse or vanish,"
it having been revealed to me many years ago
on an ordinary day in late winter.

I was home alone, probably folding clothes,
youngest child off to preschool, me restless,
cranky, interrogating God once again, demanding
to know just what was the point
of my spinning, cluttered world
—the pile of bills, the scattered toys,
trickles of water dripping from the roof,
that car I could see rounding the corner—
expecting God as usual to ignore me and
my persistent companion, Skepticism.

And as I looked out the window,
God in exasperation or my brain's synapses
bored with their more regular routes
supplanted the familiar sight of our neighborhood
with a flash vision of a long landscape:
an immense field strewn about with fallen trees, low heaps of
rubble, flattened houses, no life, and all that stood
up against the horizon were large and mysterious
shapes that I could not identify but knew,
        simply *knew*
as certainly as ever I've known anything,
to be simple acts of kindness, one person

to another, the only things real enough to remain,
to continue to exist with a life beyond their committal.

They are the real that exists beyond, and
our ultimate reality is held within them.
Tolstoy said that *a thought can propel
your life in the right direction when it
answers questions asked by your soul*,
but my visual thought that day
so far has not moved me beyond
what could be a small existence.

Dusk

Dusk claims
neither this nor that
green gives way to black
white flowers hover like ghosts
one last call from the dove that mourns

Dusk stirs
the wings of crickets
swallows swoop and dive
down the street, car doors slam
then the uneasy motor's throbbing

Dusk deceives
with its remnants of light
shadows have seduction in mind
an uncertain moon wavers on the edge
the earth's in suspension, outcome in doubt

> COMMENTARY:
> Look *behind* dusk for its mastermind.
> This daily unsettling
> passage to darkness
> meant to remind us.

Daily I think about death

I've grown sick of this obsession,
want to make a change—isn't
spring the perfect time,
when new leaves blink open
every headlong second,
to immerse in the now, follow
whatever desire's beckoned?

Impetuous birds swoop the skies
bent upon a sweet flash of
mid-flight ecstasy;
apple trees float over
our lawn, blossoming clouds;
white petals drift down to the earth,
lie there motionless (small shrouds).

PASSING

We avoid the correct word, instead
say our elderly parents have *passed*,
as though they'd gunned their old body
engines, speeding by us in one last
burst of energy, we the preoccupied
slowpokes drifting along to the side.

We want to believe they were hurrying
toward something real up the road,
not fooled by a passing mirage.

Hanging Around for God

An average sort of dog, you've
again positioned yourself at the end

of the driveway, a great spot
with its clear shot up and down

the street. Then suddenly you
think you see him—your owner!

Yes, it is him, drawing closer, maybe
even speaking. You scramble up,

tail wagging, heart leaping.
You've been watching for him

for days, years, craving contact.
And he is saying something—

but his words are babble to you,
voice not as warm as you want.

Your large dog heart sinks.
You cock your head, twitch

your ears, but still you can't
make sense of his words,

and *maybe there is no sense*
flickers dangerously

in your tiny dog mind
and you whine out loud

at the thought, unspeakable,
and because once more you're

disappointed with your owner
from whom your heart wants

a bone of love, your mind
one clear word about meaning.

You keep on listening, as hard
as you can, but it's no use.

You turn in circles,
flop back onto the driveway,

sigh a deep, shuddering dog-sigh
as your owner walks away.

*That's it! Haven't I got
better things to do with my life*

than hang around for God?
asks your tiny dog mind.

No! No! No! beats
your large hungry dog heart,

as hopeful as any dog
at even a whiff of bone.

Portraits in Time

The Past — You can't trust
that psychopath.
She'll tell you
conflicting stories,
with equal conviction,
slam the door
in your face
if you try
to prove her wrong.

The Future — You'll drop
everything at hand
to chase that charmer.
Those lidded eyes,
that tiny smirk,
his soft, honey
promises
at every bend
in the road.

The Present — You dozed through
his earlier tricks:
    scarlet scarves
    pulled from a sleeve,
    white birds aflutter,
    two rabbits appear.
A pity you only
come to at the
sound of the saw.

Meditation

I was appointed to be the one with no answers. To be tricked by the weeds, who surround the flowers and devour the earth. Before I knew it, weeds changed the landscape: modified the questions, obliterated the answers. Which is why I have given up on backyard flower beds, in favor of fields and ditches dotted with starflowers and trillium and plain purpling thistles. Catch-as-catch-can will do.

I believe in this marriage. What you give me is sufficient —what you take is just right. The balance is precarious and puzzling, the joy a blending.

I rejoice in music: the flow of it, the slow of it, the pause-then-make-a-show of it. Too many have worried how it tricked bodies to dance; the real danger is the way it seizes a spirit and toys with a soul.

I thought I would be content by now, more than half a century from birth. But still I throb with hunger and call out for comfort at odd times of night.

—with thanks to Killarney Clary

Zinnias

We drive home after days at the lake,
the silence there broken
only by a faraway motor,

the pish-sh-sh-sh of a duck gliding in
on glassy water. John dozes and
I think about the world I'm heading

toward: schoolchildren massacred;
Iraqi deaths just a passing mention
before the festive ad for allergy relief.

But all along the road, both sides,
ditches are smeared with yellow-gold,
whole fields shimmy with goldenrod,

solidago waving from everywhere.
I'm slow to let it in. Who deserves
such glory? At home, the tomatoes

are struggling to change color, but
the zinnias, being zinnias, don't give
a damn: **Look! orange! hot pink!**

Over here! red!

Do what you can

As the moon rises, do what you can.
Leave the pots to soak in the sink,
wind up the hose, put away the trowel,
let the doves have the last word.
Make accommodation with the dark:
dim down your eyes
until the white peonies blaze.

As the moon sets, do what you can.
Pull close to the warmth beside you,
wind up all your final dreams,
permit the birds a rackety dawn.
Keep your eyes on the emerging
shapes of trees, and find
consolation in the growing light.

Happiness

I didn't expect
the music of
this morning's
happiness
to resound all day
last beyond supper
past the sunset
but when I turn
out the light
it's still
humming away inside
like a
Mozart sonata
in endless reprise
theme, variations
and I resist
closing my eyes:
sleep is
certain to silence
this music
that tone-deaf
tomorrow
can never
replicate.

LANDSCAPE: SELF-PORTRAIT

The inevitable announced last night, sharp
edge of authority in the forecaster's voice:
Expect a hard freeze by the weekend,

likely in the city, for certain in outlying areas.
It occurs to her she's lived her entire life
in outlying areas, even when she lived in the city,

forever holding back just a little too much
a little too long, assuring herself
she could always move in closer

if she wanted to (though if she did
would she be herself anymore?).
Not easy for her to believe as she walks

the garden, air alive with tiny insects
glinting in the soft autumn sun,
that some night soon the inaccessible moon,

hard with clarity, will lay down a killer
glaze of silver crystals, a sepulcher,
over the startled green vegetables.

But for now, lovely now, the sky holds
only an eagle, sweeping back and forth,
spiraling up, dissolving to a speck high

over the nearby river. Lucky eagle.
How she envies him his long view,
more than almost anything she wants

to see for herself why this piece of land
must join that one, understand why it's
best for the many streams to tumble

willingly into the river, become larger
in the letting go. Day after day the river flows
fast over the shifting shallows she knows

as herself, presses against the obstructionist
sandbars she erects for protection; it rushes,
once in awhile, into the deep of her, a place

not of her making,
inexplicable,
where the moon is.